For the women who made us

©2024 Subversive Media Publications, all rights reserved.

Introduction...

This is not a book. This is a speaker, to amplify voices. It's not words on a page but real, honest truths. This is our story, but this could also be your story. This is a collection for us, for your sister, for your audience of stuffed animals; for the person sitting next to you on the bus; your best friend; for the girl with whom you lost touch; or the stranger on the other side of the café.

This is for you.

Writing this has been a journey that has brought us closer to ourselves and the reality of living life as a woman in the 21st century. We started writing this at 17, but by no means have we figured it all out: this is an open hand to anyone who's going through the motions. We have tried to be as real, honest, and unfiltered as anyone can be, to show the world our perspective on womanhood through poetry. Some of it will be angry, some of it will be blunt, raw, and emotive. Some of it will be satirical and some of it won't. Nevertheless, we welcome you.

-MF, MK & NH

Preface

I would start my preface to this collection of poetry by letting you know that I am not a producer or professional editor, and I do not seek new poetic talent as a way of life. I know that some people fill their lives with this difficult work and they have to go through a blizzard of very 'ok' verse (or worse) in order to find the stuff that gives them the very difficult to describe feeling of inspiration. That's how I feel about poetry – great poetry makes you feels as if you've touched the third-rail and you get a shock of energy that reverberates through you. It might make you recoil – but inevitably it makes the lights come on, and the wheels inside your brain race around and do unexpected things...

I founded a youth group in 2016 called the Cambs Youth Panel, and I have been blessed with the opportunity to meet many talented young people – talented in so many ways. Not always writers, but computer programmers, musicians, young academic talent... all manner of gifts. A generation of young people came into the group that contained Mimie first, then Molly and subsequently Natty. These girls all knew each other in school and were teenage friends – friends in such a wholesome, mutually supportive and life affirming way. What they didn't really know is that they were each writing and creating verse. They were writing in that private, guarded and self-conscious way that tends to indicate a fear that it might ever be discovered and read out-loud.

Working on a project about gender equality and the safety of young women in schools we discovered this writing.

Each writer, one at a time, approached me cautiously to show me a poem – privately and again, without the awareness or influence of the other writer. It was slightly bewildering to receive such powerful and authentic verse in a succession of different private disclosures – and from different writers, at the same time. I actually thought I might be the victim of a coordinated spoof! I thought that it might be verse that had been written by established writers and the girls got together to punk me! It was that unexpected. But it wasn't a wind-up. It was genuine. In one piece I literally shouted for my wife to come and see and read this piece that was in front of me, and she read it and immediately started volunteering names – "Who wrote this? Was it x? Was y?". I knew it was special. My wife and I looked at each other in that way that you might expect two people to stare at each other when you found some unexpected treasure buried in your back garden.

This really is treasure. This is genuine treasure. I'm not hyping this – I just wanted to bring it out. So, I went back to them and said "You guys need to know that you're each writing poetry – and you guys need to get an anthology of your work together."

I made Subversive Media to give voice to whoever – as long as it was an honest and truthful voice. The idea is that in an era where lies become the modern currency and the accepted and anticipated norm – telling the truth becomes a dangerous and subversive act that runs against all that. Everything presented by these three wild, uncultivated poets – is sincere, it is honest and it is completely and utterly authentic. It's a modern collective of grass roots writing – and if that doesn't excite you, I don't know what will.

-*Phil Priestley*

Before You Begin...

We understand that poetry is not everyone's cup of tea, but we do hope you take the time to try and appreciate the art behind the abstract use of words, the second meanings in straight up prose, the way our structure tells a story and how it hides true memories in its depths.

We want you to appreciate that as we bring you these simple truths, we are communicating in a way in which you get to choose how you interpret the words on the page.

However, have you ever picked up a piece of art: rhyming, abstract, performed or prose – taking a second to form your own thoughts and creating connections between your memories and theirs, before wondering exactly what brought them to put those letters on that page in that order or those brush strokes in that formation or each step to that beat of the music? Then finally resigning to the fact you'll never truly find out?

Well, we wanted to tell those curious minds what they wanted to know.

We still appreciate though, that sometimes the joy is in the not knowing. So that being said, we have placed these explanations at the end in an Author's note.

As we wrote in our introduction, this is your story. As cliché as it sounds, we want you to appreciate it in your own way. Please take your pick:

Turn each page and only read when you reach it; turn there now and study each poem with extra understanding; flick to the back after every final line or hold onto your academic pride and rip the page out entirely.

Your choice, your call. We only ask that you enjoy it.

-MF, MK & NH

Our Poems

Faces On My Wall, Which To Pick	13
A modern woman	15
ykyk	37
Dear Sir	39
An endurance test	51
I Swear I'm Not Airing You	55
One conversation	57
she doesn't talk much	59
Inertia	61
Withdrawing. dot. dot. dot	67
To drown and live	69
Broken by proxy	73
lousy grey skies	75
An ironic sonnet	77
Afraid to feel	79
Period three	81
I know a girl	85

Profound And Different	91
Carefully calculated	93
Skin	95
A Hotel Room.	101
A frantic letter	103
Pins and needles	105
Butterflies	113
bystander	115
Mirrored blade	117
Coffee and cake	119
Tall Grass	127
Trust no one	129
Window shopping	131
Another candelabra	137
Man > nature	139
You are a woman	141
Voices	145
A silent game on a board made of glass	147
Blurry Grass and Daisies	149

Love	151
A letter to my little sister	153
A sacrifice on unknown terms	159
Beautiful ludicrousness	161
windy days	167
Dandelions	169
My Granddad: A poem	177
Mind blank	179
Healing	181
Harsh design	183
calloused fingertips	185
Love Reconceived	187
Recovering reflections	189
Finality	191
Verbatim	195
A note from the authors	197

Faces On My Wall, Which To Pick

Looking up, I see them all, all the faces I can wear

One for rain, one for dances and one that's fairly rare

A red-lipped dame with sultry eyes, to bring the men to her side

Or a battered old thing, with a crooked smile that enamours all, it melts the mind.

Gruff and scruffy, intimidating grin, maybe that's the face that's sure to win.

Prize pupil star, clean-shaved and on-par with a smile that entraps gaggles of women.

Perhaps people prefer the pink-bowed daisy with an innocent gleam in their eye,

Sunkissed cheeks and a blushing nose, compelling who to sigh?

My personal favourite, a mirror facing up, to reflect heaven's beauty- it's sweeter than syrup.

Not a fanbase in sight but collective awe as they pass by, gathering hearts in an envelope,

I look up and wonder: "which shall I be today?"

"how do I decide?" "when will permanence stay?"

It's simple and confusing but I love them all the same

All my faces on my wall and no labels to change.

A modern woman

A modern woman

is a nuanced creation that takes time to perfect.

a delicate recipe,

tainted and tangled at each step,

passed down through generations

to be bottled by boys but

brewed by their fathers so

they are blameless:

A 21st century masterpiece.

Warning: contains poison

Step 1: Start with a woman

No

It begins earlier than that.

So, you must start with a child.

Because although society claims to have covered up its cracks,

behind layers upon layers of

lies reapplied,

in which they cry

"sexism doesn't exist anymore",

"we live in a matriarchy"

why,

then,

do these splitting seams

still

splinter and scratch away at the innocence

of a baby girl right up

until

she is red and raw

and reduced to no more

than body parts to be claimed

by men who feel at their most powerful

when they have a woman

by her hair

or their hands forced down

her underwear.

They don't care

that this is misogyny buried so deep,

carved so permanently that it normalises

this shame she will carry,

pain she will grow with,

for the rest of her life,

aching more than anything that bleeds,

just for being a

she.

She can't reverse

this curse:

this evolution,

this mangled reality

in which being a woman

in this modern world of 'privilege'

means that she must live in a

culture where the

measure of her femininity is in the

number of men that catcall her in the street

or touch her up in a bar.

This is a modern woman

So, step 1:

start with a child.

At school, tell her

"you cannot wear that skirt because it will distract the boys,

Skirts are an invitation" and

"reporting misogyny makes you a snitch,

and no one likes a snitch"

And tell him

"don't be such a girl, yeah, man up"

so he is moulded to believe

that femininity is small and girls

are submissive and weak,

and asking for it if

they're wearing a skirt or unable to consent

this rat race he runs in dictates that

possession of a she equals success

and so, he will grow to

know that no means yes

and she is valued less

than her violated flesh

Harsh tangibility erodes childhood fantasies,

This is a modern woman.

And when she walks home on her own

She will take out her phone

"Hello?

Where am I?

On the high street

Near the skate park

I'll be home in 5 minutes – I swear

Yeah,

I can see the house from here

I Love you

Bye"

But that's a lie

She hangs up on silence

Stale, slumping, stifling silence

This conversation is not her first but one

she has rehearsed

time and time again

because she still has a bus to catch,

there's no one on the other end of the phone

and she lives alone

miles away from here

but her fear of him is

all-consuming,

and she can hear his

footsteps behind her getting

louder,

closer,

faster

and she is scared.

She has heard the stories

She knows what happens to women in the dark but

lying will keep her safe.

"Don't worry" we tell her

It's just a stereotype

Because if her location is on then she won't get hurt, right?

If she puts her keys between her knuckles, she can fight

back against an attack

and she'll be okay if she pretends

to call a friend

because it will send

the man behind her a message that

"someone is worried about me,

someone knows where I am so if you hurt me

- you won't get away with it"

But he'll get away with it

He always does.

Because more than 86% of women

and non-binary individuals

between 18 and 24

reported having been harassed

by men

in public spaces

at some point in their life

1/3 of women experience domestic violence

So look forward to that,

but still, this is normal.

And doctors in certain parts of the world

can get 99 years in prison for performing

a life-saving abortion on a woman who is dying

but a man only gets 6 years for

raping an unconscious woman

behind the dumpster of criminal justice

where less than 2% get convicted

but this is just 'what happens'.

When you are a woman

so shut your mouth and be

grateful for the attention.

Grateful that someone is interested in you.

This is step 2.

Tell her to speak up about these things but when she does,

Tell her she is attention seeking and

She is manipulative and

she is a liar.

So she will learn to be silent.

that silence is feminine.

This is a modern woman.

And now she's eighteen and grown up

even though she grew up a long time ago

Step 3 is her first 9 to 5

but it's all she can do to survive

this constant

erosion of the shell she wears

to protect her from

this:

9am: "hey baby, you're pretty"

Where did they find you? Page 3?"

10am: "You must've slept with the boss

to get that promotion"

11:00am: a "clever girl" from the

manager when she helps a

customer

And at 12 he says:

"you'd be prettier

if you were thinner"

Lunchtime: someone's hands touching her top

Even though she asked him to stop

in the staffroom where at

3, she's asked "why are you angry?

Oh,

it's because

you're on your

period

isn't it?"

4pm: mansplaining finances because he

assumes she's stupid

"this is too complicated

for you"

she's humiliated and at

5 as he sees

her pack up to leave:

"good job sweetheart"

Sweetheart?

She shrugs it off

Remember silence is feminine

"Don't start an argument"

"It's just a compliment"

This is their game

Their rules

And you have to play it

otherwise, you'll lose

But she's already lost because she's

living an existence of sexual objectification

repackaged as female empowerment.

This is a modern woman.

Then, it's what they call 'best years of your life'

Yeah, right

"you should be out having fun"

they say

"clubbing

scared of nothing"

then why is her heart thumping in her chest

Step 4 is fear.

Concentrated fear added liberally,

generously until it spills over

And overwhelms.

He smiles.

She pushes him away.

He puts his arms around her waist.

This bitter taste

In her mouth

She's choking.

She can't see.

Memories melt and now

she can't move.

He unwraps her.

No is no longer enough.

Because it's no until you can't say it

and then it's yes

So, he drugs her so that

no means nothing anymore.

She is stripped of herself.

Slashed skin but the wounds bleed more from within

and because these bruises

will fade,

people will think that she has made

peace and moved on

but what about the bruises inside her mind

amplified each time she opens her eyes

This is step five.

Step five is being told that she lied

and that she should be able to forget.

Broken skin sews, wounds heal,

so why can't she?

And so, every day she tells herself

Over

And

Over

Again

that it didn't happen.

That her trauma is a cliché

But this is not okay

he's getting away

with it all

again.

We are still living in a patriarchy because

he should be in prison but instead

she is the one imprisoned

in shame and pain,

driven insane by the blame she is encaged in:

"you were drunk"

"you should have been more streetwise"

"You were dressed like a slut"

What did you think was going to happen?"

"You should have said no"

"Remember, skirts are an invitation"

"You wanted it"

"You're being dramatic"

This is sick.

This is a modern woman.

So, start with a child.

Follow the recipe

normality matured in brutality

and you end with a modern woman.

And this modern woman is

A woman who is told she is weak.

A woman who is told she is too sensitive.

A woman who is told that speaking out

makes her too loud,

brash,

unattractive.

A woman who knows that silence is feminine.

A woman who is defined by this

heteronormative mentality:

her identity defined by her fertility.

A woman who knows that her place will

always be at home with the kids

no matter how successful she becomes.

A woman who is frigid if she says no

and a whore if she says yes

and a woman who is told that when

she's undesirable – marked by age and

the scars of her journey

she'll become invisible.

A woman who is told that her curves make her less:

undeserving of respect but being flat means

she'll never be looked at

like that

by a man

because her femininity is not

enough to them.

A woman who is ugly

if she dresses comfortably

but asking for it if she shows some skin

A woman whose weight equals her worth

A woman who has been damaged since birth

A woman who has watched the female body degraded

to such an extent that her society accepts and

normalises the abuse and sexualization

of her gender

A woman who is violated.

A woman who is vulnerable.

A woman who is silenced.

This is a modern woman.

They say "not all men"

And we know that

But how are we supposed to know which men

Because predators don't wear a badge

and rapists don't all look the same

We've had enough of this blame

Why are we being punished?

You tell us

"Boys will be boys"

Yeah?

Well maybe it's time for you to grow up

Our bodies,

our sexualities,

our identities:

We

are not the punchline for your dinner party jokes

Or your punching bag for when you feel emasculated

You need to be educated

That skirts are not an invitation

That we are not possessions to be used or

bodies to be abused

That

no

means

no.

My body, my choice and I did not choose this.

And we know that men are abused too

This taboo is a devastating issue

But we are not trying to devalue

What you've been through

and using those words as a weapon

to invalidate her pain also invalidates his.

It tells him that he is only a victim when

a woman needs putting in her place.

Silence is not feminine.

Disrespect is not masculine.

This misogyny damages us all

But it's her who takes the fall.

Her who is buried under a blackening morality

Where her abuse is our normality

and society's silence is her reality.

This can't be allowed to fester,

to degrade her further

Step six is accepting all of this

can't be fixed

and we refuse to submit to it.

So, you have to start with a child

Go back to step one

To educate means to liberate

us from this weight

We are carrying

Teach them that sexism should not happen,

misogyny should no longer become common,

assault is not okay,

And men should never get away

with catcalling you in the street

or touching you without consent.

We have to rewrite the recipe

to strip away these lies reapplied,

these cracks they claim have covered

And start from the ground up.

We are not powerless.

We are not less-than.

We are not fragile.

These modern women will not be silent anymore.

iykyk

That word is definitely made up, but then again

Aren't they all?

A string of letters, an anagram perhaps

Wdym you're asking me?

Silly little phrases, too lazy to spell

It is easier, tbh.

Serious conversations, pepper in some spice

Srsly, what else would we do?

Secret code only we know

Idek what we're saying anymore…

Snippets overheard but never deciphered

Might as well write a dictionary atp.

Side glances and whispered definitions

It's the ageing for me.

Using words you don't know the meaning of

It's okay, I'm just in my delulu era!

Who knows how it came to be

Iykyk and that's the tea

Dear Sir

Dear Sir,

I need an extension.

    ...backspace...

Dear Sir,

I am really sorry to email you so late,

but I really need an extension,

    ...backspace...

Dear Sir,

I am writing to ask if it would be at all possible

to have an extension

on the English homework

due tomorrow

    ...backspace...

due tomorrow

please

as I haven't had enough time to finish it

    ...backspace....

as I am struggling to understand it,

    ...backspace...

As I just can't do it and

I have six other essays due by Monday and

my brain is so full it feels like it's swelling and

everyday feels like Groundhog Day, the same

thing over and over and

I'm just so tired.

Did you know that school is sick, Sir?

The education system – did you know it's making us

sick?

A little bit at a time,

degenerative

if we were using the scientific terms

You see, those kids who hand in assignments on time and

carry A*'s in their back pockets,

they are good organs

in a failing body

they are the outliers,

the anomalous results

you might say

the ones who fit through the meat grinder

and even they

are struggling so Sir,

how are the rest of us

supposed to stand a chance in a system where

the first thing you learn is your A to Z

and the second is how it is directly proportional

to your worth as a human being?

A to F, one to nine –

these 123s and ABCs are the only things that matter.

Dear Sir,

I can tell you that A is for adequate

which is an adjective meaning barely satisfactory

because I've come to learn that

an A is only adequate because

I'd be worth more if there was a star,

why isn't it an A star?

I can tell you that adrenaline is released from your adrenal medulla

and an acute angle is less than 90 degrees

I know about a squared and b squared,

that 'To be or not to be, that is the question',

and that Barak Obama was the first

black president of the United States of America

I know about cytoplasm and chloroplasts and coastlines that have

    constructive waves

D is for the deposition that occurs on those and for

Dickens who wrote David Copperfield

But when it comes to E, Sir,

I know that it's not enough

I am not enough

for them to be impressed even though

for some of us

just turning up to class each day

is an academic success.

'Children are elastic' –

they adapt and they stretch

but Sir, what about the ones who snap?

Now I know my ABCS, next time

please don't sing with me.

Dear Sir,

I told you these numbers and letters,

they're making us sick.

But don't worry.

If you feel sick

you can leave a lesson to go to the nurse

but she'll just patch up your panic attack with a blue paper towel

And send you back to class

because the second question she asks

after 'what's wrong?' is always

'What lesson should you be in now?'

'Oh. You must be trying to skip that maths test next period'

No, I promise I'm not

I just have a headache

that's been going on for thirteen years.

'I've wasted time and now time doth wastes me'

Slowly damaged.

Dear Sir,

Did you know that they weigh kids in primary schools now?

You take off your shoes and socks and stand on the scale

Where they smile or sigh

– a simple pass or fail

Visible to your twenty nine other classmates who watch

Silently, intrigued, all learning to judge

in the first round of the Hunger Games that

Some will play lifelong

It begins here.

And then they send letters home to parents

Which are stuck up on the fridge next to the

Report cards and party invitations

a certificate of congratulations or commiserations

telling them whether their child is an acceptable size,

palatable, according to a government computer

OCR, AQA, BMI - Kids are measured in all ways now.

Dear Sir,

'This is the silliest stuff I've ever heard'.

Another Shakespeare reference for you,

In case you missed the first one

a minimum of three quotations per body of writing, Miss said

it's muscle memory now, ingrained deep

I wish other things came as naturally

as that and $Y = MX + B$

like having the confidence to ask for an appointment with

the GP over the phone

or knowing how to pay a gas bill or

decipher a bank statement or

measure out your Dad's prescription

You see, school doesn't teach you those things Sir.

They weren't on the exam so why would they ever be important?

I have learned to know

not to look after myself.

I have learned to aim for perfection

and that being a straight A student is

the only way I will ever get anywhere

in life

That there is only one right answer

that you should raise your hand for,

that you always have to sit down

instead of stand up

That one size has to fit all

That it's about memorising

That when it comes down to it

Passing is more important than learning

And cheating is better than failing

That anything less than 100% attendance is laziness

Because no one cares if you can't get out of bed in the morning

You should be in school.

You should always be in school.

Dear Sir,

Did you know that in my 14 years in the British education system,

I have only ever studied one book by a black author?

I've never studied any LGBTQ+ history modules

or the biology behind disability and how

it affects people physically or mentally

we could've learned that in PE

but instead diversity is still stuck

at the bottom of our lesson plans.

Why aren't we learning about more

things that actually matter?

Why aren't we taught about different learning styles and

talents, ways of life and ways of teaching?

That school doesn't work for everyone and that's okay,

it doesn't make you less than.

Why aren't we undoing the fact that our educational system

is based on assigning ranks to everything

so that we all come to learn that some jobs are better than others and life must be lived like a race?

In fact, why aren't we trying to do undo this whole thing?

This mess.

Dear Sir,

I'm sorry for asking so many questions.

For blaming you when it's not your fault.

I know it's not your fault and

I know that

you already know all of this,

you must see it – live it - everyday.

I know there's a set

set way of doing things set out above all of us

That the expectations of students and staff alike

are crushing in a system where there are whole

chasms

Cracks cracking continually

Callously

ever wider and deeper

creating gaping holes to trip and fall through.

I get it's the system that's the problem.

The system exhausting us that we are both powerless to change.

I'm sorry.

I know this is the way it is

but I wish it wasn't.

I guess

I just wish

Someone

would change

the fucking system.

    ...Backspace.

Blank page.

> Dear Sir,
>
> I am writing to ask if it would be at all possible to have an extension on the English homework due tomorrow
>
> please
>
> as I am unwell.
>
> Kind regards,
>
> Everyone and no one.

An Endurance Test

Life is an endurance test,

A constant competition,

To see who can withstand the pain,

Who can remain on their feet,

For the longest without gain,

Flying high while your head spins,

Making sure you can maintain,

A simple smile to keep in line,

The thoughts that rush fast through your brain.

Life is an endurance test,

The kind that eats away,

At every beat within your chest,

Cutting your heart strings,

Daring you to protest,

Throwing around simple words,

And burdening you with theft,

To hold the words would make you scream,

But to blurt would further force arrest.

Life is an endurance test,

Of clever thoughts and a floating best,

To be or not is not the only question,

And you learn it hard,

That to be is barely even a suggestion,

A constant weight to pull you down,

Or a grip to hold without intention,

You can never really question where or what or who and why,

Just hold yourself up and always stand for attention by.

Life is an endurance test,

A simple ask you can't refuse,

One that never seems worthwhile,

The insurance always must be paid,

Or else all ends leave your smile,

You must follow each and every rule,

They insist you must be versatile,

Don't let them see you falter,

Instead a list you must compile,

Of all the reasons you must not fall,

Or else a fail you will find,

I mean, its never pretty when one dies.

I Swear I'm Not Airing You

Heart races, music slows

Nonsense lyrics or funny shows

Excuses made but screen still lights my face

I swear, I'm not airing you

Insta posts, multiple comments

Tiktok feed and Twitter torrents

Locked in, no out, don't want to escape

I swear, I'm not airing you

Passing laughter, many friends

Half-shut door, nearly the end

Watching time go, I'm missing something great

I swear, I'm not airing you

Overlapping sounds, too-sharp senses

Covered bases, I know all my exits

Planning my escape well before I enter

I swear, I'm not airing you

Cushioned ears, filtered noise

The perfect corner and yet another choice

Turned off phone: I'll close my mind

I swear, I'm not airing you.

One conversation

It took one conversation to make a friendship thick as thieves,

One conversation to bring a relationship to its knees,

One conversation brought everyone out in a fight,

But one conversation could last all through the night.

Words are a constant,

They can hurt like sticks and stones,

Or make happiness run through your bones,

They can create contagious smiles,

That go so far and run for miles,

A network of connection,

Constantly wired,

Without that one conversation the world would be silent,

It could so quickly turn to be violent,

So that one conversation should always be had,

Don't wonder if with it things could go bad,

Because the fruit will be sweeter if you choose to bite,

There is no point in wondering what could have been or might,

When the world turns so quick,

Just live your best life.

It took only one conversation to create a friendship thick as thieves,

And oh can't you see now what conversation achieves.

she doesn't talk much

Laughter, but only I can hear it

Opinions the voices in my head drown out

Eyes on me to say a word, I'll smile instead

Sentences drowned out because I guess it's not that interesting

Expecting the unsaid, I don't hear at all

Voice losing volume, lack of use can do that

Familiar handhold, I'm alone among friends

Too busy wondering, won't question the quiet outside

Too in my head- what was the conversation?

Full-blown worlds, why the hell would I leave?

Disappointing situations, but that's how it goes

Looking for something that was never even there

Am I just lost... Am I beyond repair?

She can't talk, she won't talk

She doesn't talk much

Inertia

Inertia: a tendency to do nothing or remain un-

changed.

That feeling of standing still

when everything else around you is dancing

to a song you can't hear.

The state of being stuck and static and

just out of

step

like a waltz with four beats or

a book with no bookshelf.

In my physics lessons at school,

inertia was: 'a property of matter that continues

in its existing state of motion or rest

until that state is changed by an external force'.

It applied to children on skateboards and footballs and cars

but not to me

because I believed,

in my preciously breakable naivety,

that the future I had so carefully

crafted for myself was a certainty.

But then again,

I always got the answers wrong in physics.

I am a caged bird now,

my wings

clipped, un -

able

to fly, feeling as though

I will forever be fixed in this nest, un -

moving

but simultaneously slipping backwards

because there is friction

between my immobility and the un-

relenting

forward motion of this modern metropolis.

There is no time to breathe, to rewind, to relive again

the times I was well

so I grieve my existence.

I envisaged something so different for myself:

aspirations rose gold and rigid and tinted with a

fairy-tale glow that

a young girl's dreams often are, now un-

ravelled by blood pressure machines and

blue paper curtains.

This is not the life I thought I would have so I

hide it away, un

seen

and whilst they

post stories of theatre trips

and university open days, proms

and picnics in the park,

someone else posts blue appointment letters

through my front door because I am

living a truth of needles and prescriptions, plates of un

eaten

food and wheelchairs in hospital corridors: an un -

well

truth that is truly un-

certain

and un-

fair

and I know that if they saw this story,

my story,

 it would make them un -

comfortable.

I suppose inertia, in that sense,

is not a tendency,

to do nothing but an

acceptance

of an inability to do something

until the circumstances around you change,

the feeling of being left behind,

a reliance on conditions external in nature

because society lets our ability dictate our worth and our story.

But we forget

that having wings that are clipped

does not mean that we will never be able to fly –

it just means that our direction,

our wingspan,

and the height

we are jumping from

may be different to everyone else's,

and whilst that is okay,

it often takes us a little longer to realise it.

So, although this is not the life

I had planned for myself, it is

unique

and beautifully so,

and I am determined to thrive in it, nonetheless.

Withdrawing, dot, dot, dot

Only ever speak to the tune of the many

Forget ever having a mind of your own making

Slowly but surely you're losing yourself in

The star-studded version of a brighter smile and wider grin

Blank stares, chaos mind

Whiteout overused you don't remember your answer

Maybe this time, you'll get it right

Unlikely story in this chapter

Don't break character, you know how that usually goes

Don't care if you're not there, guess no one will know…

Tired and sullen but they can't figure it out

Memories missed as friendships face drought

Shrink in, shrinking: this world is too big

Stare in the mirror and practice

Remember regret's a form of malice

Watching, taking in everything around

No one notices, you'll never make a sound

Thinking, thinking, rock bottom's a place to dig

Withdrawing.

dot.

dot.

dot.

To Drown and to Live

A preface:

The words before you are not a poem, rather prose. Something new perhaps, my preferred medium in fact.

I believe the following to be pathetically beautiful (if I do say so myself). The words on the page are pretty and carry a story that is not. Tragically poetic, the beauty in pain. Do not panic, I am alright. It is simply a persona and a story.

It speaks as a monologue to a love. Simply a desire to live or to not live. The confusion of breathing. Wrapped up in complicated strings of words. Read them and feel that passion or weep at it. Words are a powerful form of expression and I want to learn to hone them as a perfectly perfected skill.

With such emotions so unrenowned, I wish for my desires to stay silent. My heart should stop with that final thought. A breath upon a still water if you will; as to not disturb of course. I would rather that I should cease than for me to commit much further turmoil. This is a weight I cannot continue to carry, an ultimatum I do not wish to bare you. With that I run. I flee life in a way one may leave their home at their coming of age. You know it well my love, I know you have felt the need... to run. In a way in which one knows requires absolutely no running at all. It is simply another escape, one in which air should leave the lungs. Simple really, it failed to work absolutely when it came to my first breath so I believe it is fitting this should be my last. I cannot put into words; the truth of how I feel. I just know that I already feel as if I am drowning. I cannot come up for air. I simply do not know how. I will not ask for your assistance, only for your love I suppose as I move on. I wish for you to move on. Be careful with me, my love, I am wary; wary of you and of myself. Not of us together, not a combination, just the simple act of standing side by side. Metaphorically. Of course. I mean it all is. Metaphorical. A dream maybe, a nightmare. The contrast between love and fear for me is minimal. Love induces fear, love learnt makes me fearful and love hand crafted by man makes me petrified: yet so differently. It is not an act I wish to speak truthfully about only simply that I must state such things in order to control my own feeling, my own breath. I wish to plunge into cold waters until the anxiety leaves my chest, I wish to feel the ice around me until all my thoughts are focused on each exhale. Each inhale to prove that I am alive, that I feel life. That I live. Ironic really, oh beautiful witty irony. To feel like one is drowning and therefore wish to drown. The act of drowning allows for one to prove that they can swim so I suppose that that simply means they do want to exist. More than that. They want to feel appreciated in a way that makes them surface, to float, to swim. Safety is not safe, it is dumb. I think the truth is simpler than that however, I think it is simply that it just refuses to show itself. The danger in its entirety is that you cannot love comfortably while fearing love. I do not wish to fear, I wish to live and enjoy living. It is my lack of breath that restrains me and writing endless words calm my every shaking breath. I write with desperation as I tell you each and every word but I swear it will conclude with one very simple thought. My lack of fear is scarce as I look for hidden answers but for now I can tell you the truth of present. Simple. True. Concise.: My love, I live.

Broken by proxy

There once was a girl whose anxieties were dismissed:

'A cup of tea and a bath and it'll all be fixed.'

They say it's all in her head,

even though she can't get out of bed,

so, she'll just waste away on their waiting list.

lousy grey skies

I'm born from crappy grey skies,

Lousy rainy days run through my veins- it's all I know

You talk about sunshine beams,

Rainbow lights trailing the streets- watch them go

You ask what colour the sky is, I reply 'grey'

Maybe you laugh, sigh with disdain

But my world hasn't been any different way

I hear tales so tall of skies so bright

Of colours and light sweeping above

But dark and dull is all I've seen

My heart beats to a tune that'll never be

Sure, I can rejoice in the dull and the boring

To exist in a world of colour

I'll never know, it'll never show…

Dark clouds envelope me: I'm home.

An ironic sonnet

"Shall I compare thee to a summer's day?"

Thou were more lovely, now your temper eats

at me until I'm slowly worn away,

June's sunset oozing over bloody sheets.

Red, black and blue: these summer skies are mine

to keep on splitting skin, I must conceal

for no one knows you craft this complex lie,

your monster lurks, now sickly smile congeals.

These august storms I hadn't seen before,

there is no silver in this thundercloud.

Lightning strikes again, rotting petrichor,

on bruised -once golden- beaches, I am drowned.

Shakespeare lied; his sonnets they were silent:

Love that bloomed sweet, it still became violent.

Afraid to feel

Feel my knees knock together,

You got my heart in a tether,

Grab your hand wrapped in leather,

And so you pull me close.

So that's where we stand,

Our feet on broken land,

The expressions still bland,

And so I then push away.

I Wait for your move,

As we dance round the room,

We're completely in tune,

And now I'm scared to breathe.

Calculate your emotions,

Drown sorrows in potions,

Steal away affectionate tokens,

And still I run from you.

They said that you wouldn't mind,

They say lovers are blind,

But I know love isn't kind,

And still you kissed my lips.

Period three

It was period three when she told me.

Last Tuesday. We were sat in one of the study spaces,

I hadn't known her very long

But we were sitting, chatting,

Just talking

about nothing in particular

And then her ex came up in conversation.

It started off as most things appear on the outside:

Glossy. A selection of the truth.

He cheated on her with someone else and

Kept it from her for a while.

She was okay about it at that point,

She said she was over him and that she'd moved on

But then, as she continued to talk,

Words trickling out from within: a steady stream

of painful truths that she had locked in a box

and kept hidden away within the winding tunnels,

the intricate web of herself

now unlocked,

she became smaller.

Still very much trapped in that place

she had lived in with him for a time,

unprocessed and weeping

into recognition.

I watched her as she relived it,

as he wore her down again

twisting narratives, playing on her fears

doing 'stuff'

taking and taking

and then taking

advantage.

And then

she said

that she didn't know

if it counted as

sexual assault

because it wasn't that bad

and they're not together anymore

so it doesn't really matter anyway

and

I told her

that if she didn't say

yes

then it absolutely was

not okay.

And at that, she went silent.

Staring at the wall in front of us both, at the clock

Ticking, him

bleeding into moments

she should have been unbound.

The realisation broke her,

right in front of me

she fractured

a little

and as I looked around

at the tables of people

with so much happening to them and

waiting for them

that they shouldn't have to endure

Exams after exams,

new marks to paint onto skin,

unopened messages.

and

little sisters at home to

raise in the way they wish they had been

I saw in them too

unopened boxes

The same fractures

All different shapes and forms

Disparate structures

But no less deep

And it made me sink a little bit

into the corners of my seat...

I know a girl

I know a girl.

She smiles so no one will know,

The turmoil inside her mind,

That little thought niggling at her constantly,

As she fights to be perfect all of the time,

But no one is perfect.

She wants a good job, a good life, a good love.

To make her father proud.

She finds hope in song lyrics,

And attaches them to memories like captions to polaroids,

But she can't commit to the same thing forever,

And it's a fear she can't vocalise,

Not properly, not ever,

Because throughout her life,

She has built up to be torn down,

She had fake love once,

        but he "Broke her"

He said words,

To manipulate her world,

So she felt she could never leave him,

But its okay,

        because no meant no

But only for a little while.

His hot hands on her waist,

Passion between their lips,

And then his hands slide down

But it's fine

He won't do anything

He doesn't want to

but then passion turns to friction,

As she pulls his hand away,

And it hangs at his side,

And its honestly fine,

Because it stays,

But only till the next time,

And she feels guilty because,

He wants to give her pleasure,

And now she's unhappy and he is upset,

And then time ticks by,

Now finally she decides,

To pour out her life,

Let her smile slip,

Show her insides,

And try and talk about her mind,

And they pretend to hear,

But they're not available to listen,

And so she's just saying words,

Pretending to be heard,

And her world is controlled again,

When they say, 'I can't tomorrow',

She's cool, she smiles,

But when she says, 'I'm sorry I am not free',

She is hated and manipulated,

Into believing she has done wrong,

'I've had a bad day',

Is met with 'mine was worse',

She leans on them for support,

To be pushed back and to hit the dirt,

To contort,

Herself into the space she feels she needs to fit,

She is told, she is looking for a fight,

So they can feel victimised,

And now she is the villain,

But she's still their 'one in a million',

So when she says, 'I'm sorry, I can't do this anymore',

She is screamed at and hated,

But told,

They would be elated if she just didn't leave them alone,

And so she stays,

Until she breaks,

And then she is just one in a million pieces they hate.

And all of this rolled into one would be a clear red flag,

But when all of the acts dotted through romances,

End up like roses,

With one dead thorn.

You don't notice the damage that's done,

Because she looks pretty,

And because she might brighten up the room when she smiles,

But all of that trauma,

Now is thrown back at her,

So she's scared to confide,

Scared to love or be loved,

She'd rather run blind,

Into the sun,

Than let everyone know,

How scared she is to live life.

She's a romantic scared of romance,

Scared to get close,

She feels her breath bubble in her throat,

As the idea of committing to a job,

Just sounds like a joke,

And so she tries every day to realise,

She can be okay.

She can break the cycle,

She can fight,

To be alright,

And now she is starting to believe,

That she might.

Profound And Different

"I love you," they say

And your heart stops.

Mind racing, sweat forming- start the clock

While they sit there and stare and all you can think is 'beware'

Beware and be scared, and it's all too much to bear

So you run.

"You're kind," you hear

And immediately fear,

Fear the same story, another chapter,

Face the rapture of cruel words, a cruel world.

But you smile and you stay silent.

You don't accept it, instead despise it

You look away.

"Where did you go,"

You get questioned and interrogated with

Blinding lights and perforated stomachs, clutched in agony.

It's getting hard to breathe

And still you see a smile for you- a beam

Of hope but you can't reach it.

Clench your fist.

So you run and you look away

And clench your fists until the day

It isn't so hard to say 'okay', to believe

The words you hear them say

You'll plant your feet and stand your ground

And one day find yourself finally found

And find the meaning- something profound

You'll find something different.

Carefully calculated

Fresh taste of coffee and mint,

The metallic tang of blood as you bite down too hard on your lip,

Hot upon cold,

The burning sensation of nerves,

The loudest silence you've ever heard,

The windowpanes cold with rain,

Yet filling the room with sun,

Salt on skin, tea in hand,

Memories flashing so fast you can barely stand,

Swift movements,

Graceful and perfect,

But inside your stomach is churning,

Life is a performance,

A recurring occurrence,

You carefully calculate each one of your flaws,

Because on this stage,

Mistakes get no applause.

Skin

7:25am.

I really ought to get up now.

The laboured groans of my alarm clock ricochet off of closed walls

as today reaches in through the gap in the curtains.

I pull out my phone, the same Instagram page is open

from last night when I vowed to start loving myself:

~~'5am productive morning routine.'~~

~~She wakes up and stretches and tells herself she is beautiful, she is powerful.~~

~~She feels comfortable in skin-tight leggings~~

~~and full on avocado toast, overnight oats and~~

~~'hot girl summer' hashtags that ooze into every corner of~~

~~her feed – images eating away~~

At me, I wish that could be me.

The smell of burnt toast follows me up the stairs,

messy floor, messy hair,

~~but she says: "it's not messy", you must feel good about your natural curls all of the time."~~

~~She says "you're not fat, you're beautiful" to one~~

~~and "are you sure you're eating"~~

to me through the screen.

~~She says body positivity is power~~

and it is really,

~~She says it is healthy to commit to loving myself every day~~

and so, I turn to face myself,

to tell myself

"I...."

                      The mirror swallows me whole and now I am

                      confronted with unadorned tissue and

                      skin:

           the casing that has been my companion since birth,

           humble and blotted with blemishes I can't count

                      because I would run out

                of fingers and toes halfway through.

              Moles mottled across reddened cheeks,

           peach fuzz legs, cellulite, and acne scars.

Multi-coloured, melting pigments drawing patterns across
stretch marks and birthmarks and
freckles dappled under blistered skin.
These blemishes are what make me so strikingly myself,
but I can see them all staring back at me

and I do not feel beautiful.
~~She says I should not call these 'imperfections', instead~~
~~spots of beauty that make me unique~~
but some days it is hard
to love myself unconditionally
when society is enveloped in double standards
and dichotomies.
So, I bury the real me
beneath
layers of plaster and contour and pretend puppet giggles.

Oh, how much the skin endures.

I peel away parts of me and stitch up this patchwork

with pieces of someone else

~~She tells me that if I tell myself I am beautiful every day~~

~~I will start to believe it~~

But the truth is, we are strangers,

like two ships passing in the night,

Yes, body positivity equips and empowers

but this constant pressure to feel confident

and gorgeous every time you look in the mirror

is poisonous because

now it has gone too far the other way:

her appearance becomes her worth and

positivity becomes choosy, selective.

She is not real.

                                        Mirror, mirror on the wall,

                  why do we break so much to be the fairest of them all?

When these scars on skin

paint pictures of places we have been

and battles braved within,

like the disability they fight constantly

or the pain she has learnt to live in.

This body is just the cover to a book still being written where

imperfection is powerful because

these marks draw maps

of what I have grown to be.

I don't always feel beautiful

but my body,

as damaged or seemingly 'imperfect' it may be,

is a vessel that can create

beautiful things.

It is only part of me,

It is not the thing that gives me substance.

A Hotel Room.

It's perfect, a hotel room

Symmetrical, nameless halls wrap me in security as

I live in a space where no one is any the wiser of my existence.

Simple bliss, like a transcendent being looking fondly upon the living.

I want to stay in a hotel room,

where there's no past, no future, just now.

Find me that permanent impermanence: I want to exist in that space.

Don't let me be Goldilocks in this play,

Starring: Life, as those bowls of porridge.

I want to find one that's just right.

Not familiar, but not strange- just right.

That is a hotel room.

A universal, sensory memory foam of too-tight duvets

and mini shampoo/conditioners you can't not steal.

In a hotel room, it's lemon fresh.

Soundless greetings to neighbouring strangers and

conversations overheard that everyone can hear, but no one will mention.

The mutual agreement of unconditional silence,

minus the six-month-old who needs a nap.

I want to stay in a hotel room and live life like it's a European flick from my POV.

A Frantic Letter

Dear whoever it may concern,

It is a matter of dearest urgency that you must unfurl,

A burden of mine that I must un-learn,

Of natures twists and turns un-evident,

You must then find it all as precedent,

This responsibility that you hold dear,

Like a child to your chest all unclear,

Cold and tepid opposed to burning waters,

The impossible must all be told to our daughters,

I dot the i's and cross the t's,

For that which we have held unseen,

Greatness lies in all things credible,

For that I say your timings impeccable.

And with my request so frantically hidden,

      (If anyone would ask, I shall say that I surely didn't,)

I wish you the best in all you may be,

And with that I sign,

Sincerely,

Me.

Pins and needles

Sometimes, I get pins and needles.

Not the kind you get from crossing your legs

for too long

or lacing your boots up

too tight-

those pricklings are comfortable, kind and

comfortable because they are not permanent.

I get up and take a few steps or make fists with my fingers

and they melt away like the bubbles in a lemonade.

Fizzing into stillness: they are escapable,

diagnosed and already disappearing before

you realise they were ever really there at all-

no, the pins and needles that I'm talking about are the kind

that blister.

The kind that spread like fire across petrol

exploding,

billowing smoke that blackens

fingers first, then feet

arms and legs,

whole limbs paralysed

up and down,

in and out

and then they're in my chest

with a meat cleaver to my lungs

hacking away like an unhinged butcher to a bone

or a bulldozer to a sapling.

My body becomes a cacophony

Speech shredding,

teeth clenching,

vision disfiguring,

breath stippling,

punctured

refusing to follow the proper cadence

Stomach shallow and now I feel sick.

My insides are a black hole languishing in

paint stripper and sandpaper,

throat closing around a tumour,

head aching and anchorless,

my torso heaving and peeling until I stop breathing

pins and needles ubiquitous and aching

creating a numbness that is excruciating

and then I'm out in the garden pacing up and down

in and out

unfolding, losing myself like confetti,

scattered.

Counting five things I can see,

four things I can touch,

Up and down,

In and out.

left with only black for company.

I am no longer myself, just

an existence trapped in nerves.

Sometimes I wonder what it must be like to live in silence

without your head rewinding, replaying everything

you ever said ten times as loud as the first time you said it,

or your stomach churning or

your nervous system bubbling inside your skin

up and down,

in and out,

or if anyone really lives like that at all.

Whether the constant refrain of urban palpitations and

Unnoticed green

squashed by buildings and engines.

gasping for breath

has become the soundtrack to our lives

How quiet everything would be

if we could switch off our brain.

From time to time.

And rest.

They say, when it gets like this,

that you should make your mind a photo album,

fill it with nice things

polaroids of the beach with its foam and sandcastles

green grass and open skies

a pink memory that, although is developing in a dark room,

was photographed in the colour and the light

or something that made you happy as a child

birthday cake perhaps

or hide and seek.

Three things you can hear

Two things you can smell

Pacing up and down,

Breathing in and out,

Maybe a dream you once had,

that could also work

but none of it works because

my body is having a nightmare that is making me want to step out of my own skin.

I feel swollen and simultaneously paper-thin,

like tissue torn apart

during a game of pass the parcel

when the music stops

when does the music stop?

Up and down,

In and out,

Soon.

One thing I can taste,

Pins and needles are so much more painful than they sound

For something so small, they can take so much away

but I am okay

Soon

It will pass

Up and down,

In and out,

I replaced them with poetry.

Up

And

Down.

In

And

Out.

Sometimes I get pins and needles,

but I remind myself that these pricklings that paralyse are not permanent

I get up and take a few steps and make fists with my fingers

and they melt away like the bubbles in lemonade.

Fizzing into stillness.

I am rebuilding again.

Butterflies

Butterflies are supposed to be

Exciting

Enticing

The feeling of new born love

A symbol of rebirth and change

But to me they have only ever come with nerves

Or like cycles of a wash

As the worries churn

Around my stomach.

In love, they were uncomfy

And in day, they make me sick

But in nature they are beautiful

It's a shame that that can't stick.

bystander

Bystander, the role is yours, you take the script.

Extras pass, bumping into you, but you aren't there.

Cameras look right through you; eyes meet but never find.

Words die on the tip of your tongue, don't they care?

You've definitely fucked the scene, but no one seems to mind,

Title role but they've almost certainly found a better focus.

In an extreme close-up, they blurred out your face

Because there's something more appealing, in showbiz there's no 'us'.

Looking around, you wonder whether you're in the right place,

There goes another. Past the fences, you put up –

They can see your eyes through those glass walls, you know.

Questioning if a sunset looks as good through all that baggage.

Mic checks, one, one-two, one too many times

The sound is overpowered by the wings of a butterfly.

Doomed to watch and never see, never be, recognised.

Mirrored blade

A scream from a distance,

Is still a scream none the less,

And a dagger in my heart,

Is still a knife in my chest.

Remove emotion from action,

The outcome is the same,

One you may fear,

The other you may tame.

A bow of respect,

Is still a turn of the head,

A moment to strike,

And then your opponent lays dead.

It makes you a cheat,

But you can turn a blind eye,

Because on the ground are your feet,

And your heads in the sky.

Your mind may race forward,

But it's easy to forget,

Cause action from emotion,

No reason to fret.

Betrayal may fuel you,

Just don't let your mind stop,

Cause one thought of your action,

could cause your guard to drop,

and with that you may choose to make your own heart

                            stop.

Coffee and Cake

It's a seemingly insignificant

morning in mid-July

and my friend messages me

completely out of the blue and asks

if we could go out for coffee and cake.

She says she knows a nice little place just around the corner,

It does toasties and American pancakes

Like the ones with maple syrup and bacon and strawberry sauce

everything: the whole works, they even do

hot chocolates too which is good because

I don't really like coffee

that much

we could even do lunch if I want, she says

she could pick me up,

or we should walk there

if 11 is a good time – not too early,

not too late- but then she changes her mind and

insists on picking me up at 10

because that way we'd

have more time to catch up

over coffee and cake.

She tells me it's been way too long

and she's so excited to see me

and I tell her

    I'm sorry.

    I'm sick today.

She asks if I'm free next week for coffee and cake

with a full stop instead of a question mark

so I turn my phone off

because both she and I know what is happening here

and those two blue ticks instantly become a symbol of resignation

to the fact that

it will be another year before she can amass

the strength to ask again.

I get it.

Holding somebody up who has no interest

in being held up gets hard,

thankless even.

I want to, one day, be able to tell her

How thankful I am for that, for her

over coffee and cake – how

she persevered even though I

hid myself and the truth from her

entirely and the person and friend I have

become is not a kind one.

I want to be able to tell her that truth

As well as the ugly, unromantic, acidic truth at

the core of it all

that I am happy when I am empty

and I cannot breathe when I am full.

I used to sit next to her in

science lessons at school,

that's how we met.

We weren't really good at it

back then but she got better

and became a doctor whereas I got worse

and became a patient.

I want to be able to tell her that

I'm scared to see her

because nowadays if anyone asks

me something, I don't really know what reaction you're going to get

Because I'm a little bit unpredictable –

a haphazard hypothesis, a failed experiment

that I thought was working because everyone

said the results were right

but it wasn't right because it turns out

all that counting and dividing and taking away

doesn't make you happy,

 it just makes you sick.

I want to be able to tell her that

I've been a bit hollow.

I want to be able to tell her that

I'm tired.

I want to be able to tell her that

I really

did want to see her today.

That it's not her, it's the coffee and cake

And I just tell a lot of lies because

I am terrified

of what she might say if she knew.

How she might look at me

Differently,

sadly,

as though I am nothing

but someone reduced

to mere, unadorned vulnerability.

Newly breakable.

So I lied to her.

Again.

    I'm sorry.

    I'm sick today.

But if I'm being truly honest, I know she knows that.

She knows me too well.

All of me – my love for

melodramatic poetry and blue dresses

and the fact that I'll always take a picture of the

sky wherever I am, how I tease my sister and curse

the weather no matter what it is

and my propensity to lying, how they

they slip off the tongue

too easily for me, fluid in the absence of such.

They're gentler on the stomach.

I promise I don't mean to use them as my armour, but I do – constantly.

They protect me. I can't help it.

I'm sorry she has come to expect them.

I'm so sorry they've also become my weapon

And now they hurt her.

It's just complex lies are

sometimes easier to digest than simple truths.

for her or for me

I'm not sure I know anymore.

Tall Grass

Leaves of mystery, an enemy lurks within

I'll double-take and look again, shivers down my skin

Won't turn my back can't let them win, it can't be in my head

I worry and I worry, smelling pollen-scented dread

Greenery and shrubbery cloud nefarious desires

Beady eyes meet mine, innocence is a liar

Maybe I'm too rash, too brutal with my opinions

The eeriness deters me, they're playing the long con

Tall, tall grass, lined with creepy crawlies

I'll stay inside instead.

Trust no one

Words can mean everything,

Yet nothing at all,

Words can build bridges,

And break them down so you fall,

You can look for a safe place,

A soft place to land,

But a safe world is trust-less,

So you must endure and withstand,

Or alternatively hide far away from man.

A single word can cut deeper,

Than any blade forged of gold.

Or any shot that would encourage your hand to fold,

You must conceal from your friends,

So that your foe cannot strike,

The right words can cause turmoil,

If said just right.

Safety is always found in those more silent of a night.

If you never share your own secrets,

They can't ever see you bleed,

But a world without trust,

Is a lonely one indeed.

Window shopping

Pressing drooling faces against the panes -

glass misted - stringed saliva lights dripping,

reflecting glossy idolatry back,

they each insert a coin to play

in the arcade of glistening 'others' where

they can peruse perfected personas

that can be picked and purchased at leisure

to take home and adopt for a season.

Outside, the tinselled streetlamps cascade yellow

onto the prizes to be won inside the

multi-coloured monopoly shops:

sanguine green and red dominoed

over cigarette ends and rained on streets,

casting shadows on

empty blankets and purpling fingers

'Can you spare any change?'

The stench of paper means

these piccadilly people cannot

hear her. Actuality bookended and squashed

by gluttonous shells of shops

all hollow yet overfull

and oozing monsters moulded into men

as they swarm from frame to frame

on their hands and knees like flies

to a porch light

gorging on strawberry-lace limbed

mannequins and 'every little helps',

pine needles stuck to half price carpets,

red and white diagonals and crackling turkeys,

a bumper edition Radio Times,

icing sugar driveways plastered onto TV screens,

platinum figures posing with gingerbread kitchens and

smiling children jumping on sofas that were

delivered in time for Christmas,

regurgitated beer and cinnamon,

purses full to

bursting like bloated Boxing Day guts,

reindeer plastic bags, 20% off woolly hats,

tissue paper crowns

the bear and the hare and

the penguin paired,

a fire breathing dragon melting

slippery ice

and the man on the moon with

his telescope in hand looking down

on an earth enveloped in buying

and selling

and restocked promises

of happiness and full stomachs

that play out to sentimental music

in an advert every year that's

'Just too good to wait': all,

cloying into

an ersatz wrapped in rose gold and silver cellophane

sprinting

stuck.

Reality obscured.

'I'm not going to buy anything'

says the girl, features flattened as she presses her face

against the cold, crisp glass – drinking in

unsettling escapism,

perfection

pixelated, printed and pasted

onto a little red dress inside the

shop window.

Every day after school, she

steps into its folds

glittering pleats beautiful and still

as her silhouette shakes from the blows of the wind

making the

the edges of her coat spill out

from its unflinching outline -

it doesn't quite fit her,

reflected,

so, she trudges home - cursing her empty pockets

and pink skirt but

she'll be back again the next day

to stare at it again for hours

on end, I

watch her ache for it. She was addicted

to silver and gold

at seven years old

and this afternoon they took it off.

The red dress removed

from view, purpose fulfilled: it is no longer part of the

perfection on sale this season

now manufactured

by daisies and dungarees

and February date nights -

she is directionless, cast adrift, sinking

slowly into cruel reality.

It's cold.

'Can you spare any change?'

The stench of paper means these piccadilly people

cannot hear her.

Red dresses in shop windows

whitewash painful existence.

Another candelabra

La dee da, La da dee

I fancy me, a fancy thing,

A vah-se, not vase, of peonies or the perfect shiny ring

Here's a trick, let's count to three

Ask me what I always see

Fresh hors d'oeurves served half-hourly on my brand-new balcony

The finer things, or so I'm told

The cash it takes for real, pure gold

I'm not so sure it's quite so bold

Or old enough for me

Polished shoes are what I wish

To see my reflection in a silver dish

Or see a jet and reminisce

Of months spent abroad

I want it all, I want some more

The perfect shoe- why not the store

From what I know, less isn't more

I'll take another candelabra.

Man > Nature

It's getting darker.

Sun swallowed by swellings of smoke

Skin, sea, sky: all,

Blackening and relinquished to shadow

I am lost to coughing fits and convulsions

Floating out onto a shallow sea

Stripped bare

Of green and blue and peach

Can you hear it?

The silence.

Almost as deafening as the groaning underbelly of an urban concrete jungle

Or the thunderous roars of murderous machinery,

It massacres.

I long for the chirping of winged creatures

And the peppermint nests they build

To fill the air again

But alas they are gone.

I must be content with the silence

I helped to create.

You are a woman

'Isn't it funny,

That a pretty lil girl like you

Wants to do a job like that'

That's kinda funny

Words spoken too often:

Don't be loud, don't be cold

Just be quiet

Be confident

Be clever

Shake his hand

But not too strong,

don't come off masculine,

You are a woman.

Be proud,

but be modest,

be kind,

but not a push over,

That act was too brash,

Unless done by a man,

For you it was thoughtless,

For him it was funny,

You are a woman.

Don't let him speak to you like that,

but whatever you do,

don't speak back,

you can't wear that skirt,

or too much makeup,

it makes you a slut,

but don't cover up.

You are a woman.

The rules are complicated,

and messy and cruel,

you can't do anything

even if you want to,

you will always be asking for it,

or you got the wrong end of the stick.

These rules don't bend,

you'll just be 'that bitch'.

You are a woman.

But women are powerful

Beautiful and confident.

Don't listen to those men,

or look for the sentiment,

their words are just blank.

cold and effortless,

and I hate that we live in a world where that effect is,

powerful and played on.

You are a woman.

But we can fight back,

we ignore and unite,

react and spite,

be calm and clever,

and conquer together,

cause it's a powerful thing,

to create change unnoticed,

and the anger that comes will just last moments.

Fleeting and forgettable in the move that is change,

into a world that will be a better place.

I am a woman.

We. Are. women.

Voices

Cadent tone, fill the room with your words

Tell them all the things they've never even heard

Tell them about all the strife we're in

Tell them what's really a sin

Raise your hand in solidarity, raise your voice

Silent anger, show us who you hate

Tell us their wrongs and how we'll become great

Tell us your story; we'll stand beside you anyway

Tell us so we can make them pay

Raise your voice, lift up those who can't

Paralysing insecurity, teach me how to do better

Tell me all and we'll cry together

Tell me your demons, I'll prepare for battle

Tell me what biases to tackle

Lift up those who can't, spread the word

Unheard outrage, let us be your shield

Be the change you need and we'll show up on the field

It's a modern world, of course we're evolved

Pat us on the shoulder: all the problems are solved

Spread the word, no change behind a screen

Blind awareness, they aren't listening,

Hashtags spread, but tensions bristling

Protests great, but they all go back

Don't know what to do, too scared to attack

No change behind a screen... just raise your hand in solidarity.

A silent game on a board made of glass

If a girl said nothing,

Sat quietly aside,

Waiting to be reasonable,

Hide from cutting lines.

You'd shout and you'd cry,

Till the world heard her words,

Remove the unfairness of each and every lie,

As productive as arguing with a wall made of brick,

Enough to make your blood run thick,

To your brain.

Tears fall fast,

In screams of mental pain,

Your deathbed is raw,

Cuts her deep,

Right down to her core.

The girl is my reflection,

The one that you've seen,

Every day in the glass,

And you prep and you preen.

We are three the same,

The silenced, the angry.

Our tears act like fire,

As we continue to stare blankly,

We wipe away off our burning cheeks,

As we stand ready to play ourselves as a new piece.

Blurry Grass and Daisies

This is not a bus.

This is a chariot, racing through the fields

Because being late to a banquet is tacky.

Rolling hills and winding paths,

Sights of wonder await.

Slip away and imagine magic in the plains.

Vast forests lay before you,

They listen for your decree

Trees grow as your army does, mysterious and challenging.

Concrete roads all blur into one.

After several hours on the road, they seem

To blend together at some point.

Travelling with grey overcast,

It's your enemies conspiring against you.

The rain falls with ice-sharp precision.

Sun-aged wheat bows with the wind,

No longer at your service,

Clear skies mimic your following.

Your chariot awaits to whisk you away

From thundering steps of enemy armies.

No longer your kingdom, you rest your head on the window.

This is not a bus.

Love

Don't confuse love, from care, from a wanting to be around you, from friendship.

Don't assume it is love when it is simply a need for affection that they could potentially fill.

Do not wish it to be love so you can scrape at the desire to not be touch starved for a second longer,

To not have to crave intimacy like an addict craves their fix.

Do not mistake kindness and remembrance for love.

Do not confuse my actions for love.

You do not love me.

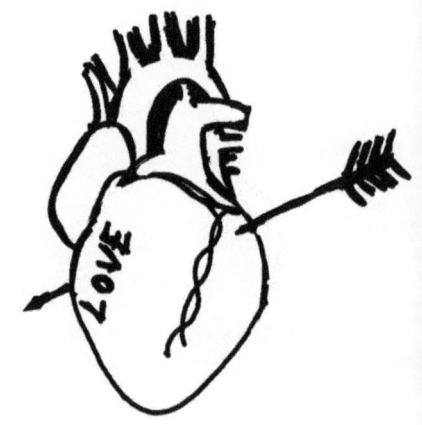

A letter to my little sister

There's a blackberry bush in our back garden –

I'm not sure if you remember it too well

as a fixture in your younger years,

It was never really supposed to be there,

They didn't plant it,

they put the beginnings of an apple tree there to begin with

but the birds had other ideas

and so now it is rather a permanent feature that

we take secateurs and spades to,

See, we dig it up most summers,

when we remember,

Because it grows too big and spreads out

And takes over, threatening to uproot the

dahlias and the box hedge

and the little tulips that Mum put in last Autumn.

Last year, we went as far as to line the soil with tarpaulin.

To stop it escaping up through the compost and

displacing Mum's acer, Granny's dahlias, Grandma's lavender, my daisies

and your roses that we planted twelve years ago now, but

its thorns are stubborn, and it reaches out and ravages regardless.

The plant is frightening,

sometimes –

in its refusal to be tamed, in its

sweeping overwhelmingness and spikes and the fact

that it grows and grows and grows

so big that some days

it feels like it might engulf the whole garden.

I get scared of it too,

the purpling earth with all its thorns.

But whilst it may try, it will not uproot our flowers

because we are sewn too deep.

Your roses, they will continue to flourish and you with them.
You are beautiful.
Beautiful and vivid.
You deserve to grow to be tall and loud, you deserve to
take up space.
Don't let anyone try to cut you down or uproot you
and know that if anyone dares,
you are special.
You were nurtured and shaped by powerful women
both past and present
who, in their strength, have made you strong too
by teaching you that you are valuable.
You hold value in your body and in your words,
your thoughts, your dreams.
Know this and believe it. It is your superpower.
Know that there are people on this earth who would go to the

ends of it and back for you and those same people

hold a love for you that is unchanging and unconditional.

Never settle.

Never lose your brightness.

Hold onto your rose gold joy always even if

it sometimes feels darkened by the blackberry shadows.

I love you, idiot.

(P.S. Do not get a fringe

unless you have thought it through

absolutely and completely

and remained consistently committed.

to the idea for at least 14 days.

The growing out process gets ugly,

And I don't mean physically.

Really ugly,

Really quickly.

And if you absolutely decide you want one, do not

  – under any circumstances –

cut it yourself.

Nothing screams 'No I did not get therapy' like a wonky fringe

Cut with kitchen scissors,

  in front of the bathroom mirror.)

Love, your idiot big sister

with a half grown out fringe.

A sacrifice on unknown terms

Turning black and blue as I lay there in the dust,

The blood rushing with adrenaline as I come to terms with such,

I know the feeling well I have always been prepared,

But I did not account for love and lust and loss within this nightmare,

I seek their touch and their care,

Their smile and the twinkle of their eyes, the shine of their hair,

With pain comes remembrance,

The shakes of new memories lost,

And though this comes with bravery, this action takes at what cost?

My selfish thoughts take over as I stare into the darkness,

The regret I swore I would not feel as I entered deep into this mess,

But it is always love that swears,

When it is the one you love that bears,

The sword that takes the final blow,

The cut that ends your blood flow,

As blood seeps out to spell out this lie,

I come to terms with my time to die.

Beautiful ludicrousness

There is a certain ludicrousness in being human.

When you think about it,

isn't it so ridiculous,

almost inconceivable that we have the ability to be both

happy and sad,

broken and whole

at the same time?

We laugh and cry and write about each other – ballads,

memoirs, love notes and hate pieces and

angry existentialisms that we wrap in hardback and

put on shelves for each other to buy and muse over, we

embrace, we destroy, we put back together and press

ourselves to one another and prize ourselves apart

in a single breath and still remain completely,

completely the same and different all at once.

Isn't that ludicrous?

And isn't it almost laughable how,

despite this shared fragility,

we still encourage the ability

to pretend that

such pure, imperfect humanness,

doesn't exist? That

we're completely normal and fine

and put together,

we put together

this façade,

we normalise,

we idolise

this painting of a picture of put togetherness

so that we can hide

from the simultaneous anxious belief that

we are the only ones who make fools of ourselves

because the real ludicrousness of being human is

the belief that that we are alone in our stupidity.

In doing so we deny our own natures: gold and silver

in their untainted sincerity.

We believe that 'It is just me

who cringes,

who winces and blushes

and groans in embarrassment

so vast, it feels,

that I want nothing more than to curl up into a ball and disappear'.

And we do this perpetually

even though the sheer essence of being human

is to panic when someone sings happy birthday to you

because no one ever knows what to do

so you just stare

at the floor while your cheeks flush red

and you think about it for hours on end

until next year rolls around again.

Being human is cheating in board games,

even though you always come last and

checking your hair in shop windows

and denying that you snore, it's

coming home after a night out and realising

that some of your lunch is still stuck in your teeth and

overhearing a joke in someone else's conversation and laughing,

a little too loudly,

sticking your tongue out

when you're concentrating

and talking to yourself without realising you're doing it.

It's singing when you think no one else is around

and returning a wave to a stranger who was actually waving

at the person behind you so you try to turn it into a something,

a scratch of the head or a stretch,

and convince yourself that you've gotten away with it

even though everyone around you knows that you definitely haven't.

Our humanness is completed by the fact that we

sit in awkward silences

and trip over our own feet.

We are all daft and imperfect

and self-conscious about all of the above

even though it is that which makes us so precious and

so unutterly alone.

There is such beauty in this ludicrous humanity.

windy days

I wonder whether if the wind could speak, it would talk to us.

Would it be a whisper, soft breath against our ear

Or a wail of all the sorrows it's witnessed?

Remembering simpler times when all I wanted to be was It.

Closed eyes as it whipped my too-big cardigan closer, keeping me warm,

and wilding out my messed-up hair in an attempt to become relative.

I'd roll alongside it's rippling waves, just trying to keep up,

Leaving school friends in the dust as I'm swept away.

Introduced to the sun, to the rain, to the snow- I'd tip an imaginary hat

and it would take me once more.

Laughing the whole time, of course, because I'd never felt so weightless;

I could conquer the world. Or so I thought, believed, maybe it was just hope?

Now my hair is neat and tied back, I don't know where that cardigan went,

My eyes are wide open, and I no longer see It in windy days.

I still wonder whether the wind would talk, but if I think about it, it always did.

Every so often, despite my age, I'd hear that familiar call.

So I would go outside and close my eyes for just a second,

transported back to simpler times where all I wanted to be was the wind.

Dandelions

In these woods, there are dandelions

growing wildly,

without inhibition

these pinpricks of brilliant yellow map out constellations

and connections within my complexion

recollections glowing,

neurons glinting in a nervous system

of leaves and trees that breathe,

exhaling deeply into a permeance of grayscale and white.

I have watched the rise and fall of expanding yellow

- a rhythmic movement of breath filling lungs-

punctuate this past for as long as recollection allows.

These veins and wrinkles were sculpted long before,

but it is these

yellow memories that mould me.

All that I am grew from the dandelions.

Shhh, make a wish.

'Please don't let me forget this.'

        I am scared of

forgetting.

But thorns graze and the cold strips

              this sunlight, these dandelion memories.

Blonde bleaches

      and whispers of white

                      wander

gently to somewhere far away...

dissolving

      in

            the wind.

Gold peeled from green.

Pieces of me

      picked from myself

like   cauterised   capillaries:

disconnected,

and

left

to

        drift.

Until I am...

...lost.

But I am not empty.

The essence of perfume lingers,

        these seeds

                float

away

        and are planted elsewhere.

      These yellow memories that were mine,

    I shared and now this rose-gold is theirs too.

I was scared of forgetting,

but these fields of dandelions, these memories

inside my head

are precious in their persistence to prosper.

They are sprinklings of gold that

line paths of timeworn joy engraved

into the skin of this forest floor.

They are the binding of this woodland,

the stitching that holds together the stretching seams

of our patchworks.

They are recollections of yellow and pink

and lavender purple,

memories oozing in treasure.

These are my dandelions.

Each flower in bloom reopens a package

of time already passed

as a trace across lips or along fingertips:

That one is for muddy wellington boots

and rain on climbing frames.

That one, over there, is for lemon meringue pie,

the one next to it for piano duets

harmonised with new-born cries

from times gone by.

The ones behind us from graduations

and ticking clocks, the tapping of

graphite against desks.

This one is for white lace and dahlias,

                                battles that were fought

                                          and won

                              but those that we lost too.

                                      And that one:

                    a precious petal, flourishing furiously,

                                         that one

                              is my Granddaughter's.

In her woods there are dandelions growing

in exquisite abundance,

yellow wildflowers spilling over,

stretching out into rolling hills of gold and green.

I wish I could see that even though disease withers me now,

she will blossom despite.

So, when tomorrow starts without me,

my dear,

when the memory of you and all that was

is taken from me and I am but a shell,

I wish for you to flourish.

To live:

>   freely,

>   wildly,

>   without inhibition.

>   Do not be scared of forgetting.

>   It is so painfully limiting when

>   There is too much life

>   Left to be lived.

My Grandad: A Poem

Fame is a thing for aspiration,

With a desire to grasp like sun needs sky,

But he, he was famous in the best kind of way,

The quiet way in which you simply exist by,

The world may not know him,

But the people who do,

They hang off each word and value him through and through,

Everyone has their stories,

And their memories too,

Oh, how he came to life,

With each voyage he embarked on,

And how he loved his wife,

everyone may know a part of him i don't,

But his memory lives on,

In a way that I won't,

He was the greatest man I've ever known,

And for that,

My pride is forever shown,

For love and lust and all things resilient,

My grandfather,

Well, he was brilliant.

Mind Blank

Words. Words. Words.

My greatest foe, my deepest love,

Words, why do you hide?

The thoughts are there, I reach through the thicket

Grasping at nothing, hands empty –

Not a thing.

Screaming into the abyss, it ought to reply sometime, right?

Wrong.

Words. Words. Words.

Twiddle thumbs and stare.

Synonym searches and the shoe never fits.

12 scenes- fully fledged- but only a lonely word on the page.

Thinking about the good ol' days, where chapters flowed with ease…

Maybe I'm getting old.

Words. Words. Words.

Flowing prose, touching words, at least so I thought;

What happened to the award-winning plot I'd written?

Incoherent sentences and inconsistent tenses- I swear I've just made up words.

People lied when they said genius strikes after midnight.

Healing

It takes a lot to share one's burdens,

To lean on another after so many falls,

To start a new chapter of a book you can't read.

It's that that I'm scared of, I've supposed, it seems.

After wondering forever, a conclusion at last,

The unknown is inevitable but my fears in the past,

If history repeats itself just mirrored on a new face,

It's that in my ideology that holds my struggle to keep up pace.

Happiness ensues but memories hold me back,

Emotion for commitment is not something I lack,

But a years worth of memories could be worth it for that,

Every person is different, no one that is the same,

and with that I find I could contain,

My hope to be happy this time around,

Because it's with that sentiment my heart can be found.

With the lit-up nights my blank page stares me fresh,

Right in the face, no ink in its depths,

A unique volume straight from the shelf,

This feeling new and exciting for no one

                                              But

                                                          myself.

Harsh design

I think that,

maybe,

      we're designed to hurt

  otherwise

how would we know

   when we are

      healing?

calloused fingertips

Do have careful hands, place them just right

Go over and over until the sound is clear

A moment will not pass when you won't feel slight

Disaster always far too near

Greatness is fought for, not found

A minor set back, get up off the ground.

Examples must be made, striving for perfection

Glad it's coming together for fear of an outside source

Enthusiastic strums fill the room with convection

Growing on you, isn't it, the musician's remorse.

Exactly 47 tries, and one more for the road

Getting sorta irritating, this must be all in vain

A final straw taken, you're about to explode

Don't fret, my dear, the next one breaks the chain.

Dreary sunday mornings, what would you do without them?
Clear, harmonious notes as time has been worth the pain
Another song in your pocket, written on your hand in pen
Down time- slow strums to the soothing, sweet rain
Calming down now, as the music comes to you
All too real, the talent is ringing true.

Chilling melodies sending shivers down spines
A morsel of sunshine in the grey
Finding a sound you now call 'mine'
Good tunes, good enough, it's all okay.

Calling out for another song to stay
Ending the moment, it's been a fun trip
A mirror to your past, you've come a long way
For what is it all but calloused fingertips.

Love Reconceived

You are so close to me. Physically.

So close our breath could be shared

but you are not mine.

Do not ever think I am yours.

Friendship at most, hatred first.

Do not use me as a gap filler of affection to cure your starve of touch.

Do **not** let me use you.

Don't **dare** scrape at the desire of me, when I am something you have invented.

Do not confuse my remembrance for love when I am merely observant,

Forcing something as you crave intimacy like an addict craves their fix,

This world could turn faster than I would ever let you in

Forcing yourself through my walls unburdened.

You scream for me **to** open up and I detest you for it.

Believing you can see my bare skin as your own flaw,

                        Something you can fix,

You break down my boundaries and leave me lying raw.

You cry to me, scream to me, only building the space I run to put between us.

Proximity. Too close. Running. Breath. On my neck.

Your words too loud pounding in my head.

I don't want you to hate me but I can't not hate you.

You have built up a lie in your head, a belief of a closeness that doesn't exist.

And that lie has shattered and now you are angry.

So listen to the words the pieces must speak:

Do not confuse my kindness for **love.**

                My actions for love.

                You do not love **me.**

And I will n**ever.** love you

Recovering reflections

There's something very special about living

a life you never thought you could have.

It is not something that you can give to words,

Not something that can be encapsulated by

The creases and curves of syllables on lips or

the undulations of simple letters,

No, this redefined existence,

where you have relearned a routine

without sickness, and limits

and 'I won'ts'

is not something that can be described.

It something you can only feel,

deep within you.

A freedom never before felt:

a fizzing, a deep inhalation, a fulfilment that comes

From simple things

Like unpunctured breath,

walks to the end of the path,

Deciding to have coffee and cake

that represent a battle

you kept hidden away

a battle that dragged you to the bottom and pulled you under

and came close to drowning you completely until

you said to yourself that there had to be more to life

than this.

They represent the day you chose to live again

And all the days, weeks, years afterwards

That you spent picking yourself up and putting yourself

Back together

Time and time again

Fighting against the parts of yourself that were still stuck inside your illness

Every step of the way

to reach the blue at the top of the mountain.

The view after it all

is so worth the climb,

I promise.

Finality

She's like a whirlwind in open air,

Lost in the moment as if she doesn't care,

Chaotically present but almost unperceived,

Trapped within the seconds almost as if no one can see,

The sand that slips through your fingers,

As it does through the glass,

But oh how she wishes this feeling would pass.

As she looks in the mirror she sees the scholar as she's seen,

But if she looks into her soul it's the terror that gives her a pale sheen,

The pallor of her skin is her only reflection to the pain behind her eyes,

Almost unnoticed like clouds that shift through the skies.

An automatic motion passed without a jury,

The quiet scream of frustrated anger emphasised by fury.

The greatness that laughs like a hidden smile,

A lump in her throat acidic from bile,

The greatest lives are ones with duality,

And now this all ends with a sense of finality.

Except nothing really ends does it...

Verbatim

Word for word,

Turn of phrase,

Another line of synonymous names,

Tell their tales,

Of their days,

Now only to be warped and changed,

Lost by time,

Blurred out haze,

Blaze of glory out in flames.

It's one truth,

Just three ways,

Not verbatim but still quite the same.

A note from your writers

What follows is our own way to try and make poetry more accessible. An explanation for our words, a thought process or an inspiration. A true answer for when your English teacher asks you what the writer intended you to think when they made the sky blue. A blurb for each poem.

Interpret what you wish within our poems, but this is an insight into what they mean for us.

We thank you for reading our carefully crafted truths, for pondering our words and we hope they meant something to you as they do for us.

Faces on my wall, which to pick
Deciding who I want to be for today. I hate consistency.

A Modern Woman:
An exploration of a young girl's life and the barriers she encounters as she grows up.

IYKYK
Expect cringiness. A poem to be read not to be heard.

Dear Sir
The email you wish you could send to your teacher.

An Endurance Test
Always having to be the best, where everything has to be a competition - graded, marked, assessed.

I swear I'm not airing you
And other lies I tell my friends…

One Conversation
Yet again about words. The power of words and how little we think about them, I suppose we're quite careless with them. About communication: if you don't try, you can't expect people to know what you're going through.

she doesn't talk much
To all the conversations I'll never have

Inertia:
Physics… and for people that feel a bit stuck.

Withdrawing, dot, dot, dot.
I don't like socialising. The end.

To drown and to live
The preface was too poetic, so it ended up in the poem.

Broken by proxy
A self explanatory limerick.

Lousy grey skies
Bad weather as a metaphor for how messed up society is.

An ironic sonnet:
A criticism of Shakespeare's over-romanticisation of love and relationships in his sonnets and how he leaves no space to portray the darker, but very real, side of finding love with someone who turns out to be totally different.

Afraid to feel
Unclear… it's something about love.

Period Three:
Inspired by a real conversation with someone i met at sixth form.

I know a girl
A story of my relationship trauma.

Profound and Different
Jokes, jokes... or are they?

Carefully Calculated
About having to be perfect all the time. Not much more to it.

Skin:
shrugs it's a poem about learning to accept your body on the days you find it harder to love. Inspired by Emma Thompson's (the love of my life) interview with Stephen Colbert where she says that there's no point hating your body, 'it's your house, it's where you live' - don't waste your time.

A Hotel Room
Hotel rooms are nice. The rest is straightforward.

A Frantic Letter
Inspired by that feeling where you can't quite figure out the words you want to say. The confusion behind trying to communicate.

Pins and needles:
A panic attack in words.

Butterflies
Half-anxiety and panic attacks, but also about being uncomfortable with people who you should be comfortable with. Caterpillars spend all that time preparing to become a butterfly, only to last for a few days. Why obsess and fret and struggle over something that will only ever be a moment frozen in memory.

Bystander
You know that emoji? The disappearing face? Well, that's this poem. Enjoy.

Mirrored Blade
Perspective. There are two sides to every story. It's about how everything can be perceived in different ways. It's called Mirrored Blade because a mirrored blade is shiny and it can look beautiful, but it can also kill you.

Coffee and Cake
It's about having a fun funky relationship with food, while trying to convince everyone you don't have a fun funky relationship with food, when in fact they're all aware you have a fun funky relationship with food.

Tall Grass
I really hate bugs…I really do. They're so creepy. *shudders*

Trust no one:
About how words are the only thing you can use to communicate, but words lie. The likelihood of your trust being broken is so high because even our tools of communication are unreliable.

Window Shopping:
Consumerism… innit.

Another Candelabra
There's a running joke in my family that i have expensive taste. And this poem is my self-awareness that I do in fact, have expensive taste.

Man > Nature
Inspiration from another day in sunny sixth form, with some stupid gap filler task so they can pretend that they've educated us properly on climate change.

You are a Woman.
A declaration.

Voices
About how we've progressed but sometimes it feels as though the progress is slowing down when we don't want it to.

A silent game on a board made of glass
There are 3 characters in this poem: the writer; their reflection; the reader. All are one person. Every experience is different yet the same. It's a silent game we play, as if to pretend we are not. The board is made of glass: you can see-through it till it shatters and breaks the façade. But at the end of the day, no matter how well we play, womanhood is a game after all, with its rules inscribed through history all written by a man. We are all chess pieces in a little game called life.

Blurry Grass and Daisies
Daydreaming on a commute.

Love
About coming to terms with the understanding that sometimes what you want or crave isn't good for you, but you convince yourself it is. Proximity doesn't equal love.

A letter to my little sister
For my little sister but also for all our younger selves.

A sacrifice on unknown terms
I suppose… it's about betrayal. About loving the person, while knowing they're going to hurt you.

Beautiful Ludicrousness
People are silly.

windy days
Based on a memory from primary school. My friend lost her hair tie. It was a very windy day and the genius that I am decided that the best way to find it was to be the hair tie. So, we lay on the grass and crawled round with the wind taking us wherever it was blowing and eventually, we found it.

Dandelions
My inspiration came from witnessing a degenerative illness. Picture yourself in the temporary state and understand and come to terms with that which you cannot control – and celebrate what remains.

My Grandad: a poem
This is a poem about my grandad.
Who ~~was~~ is the greatest man I ever knew and he shaped me into the woman I am today.

Mind blank
Writer's block, bane of my existence.

Healing
An epilogue to 'I know a girl'

Harsh Design
Just read.

calloused fingertips
Based on my experience as an instrument player. It's quite picturesque don't you think? The wear and tear of something well-loved.

Love Reconceived
Revisiting 'Love' after the moment. Retrospectively. Now the emotions have shifted and the anger has built.

Recovering Reflection
A note to recovery.

Finality
It is what it says on the tin. It's about the end.

Verbatim

verbatim

adverb

1. in exactly the same words as were used originally.
   "subjects were instructed to recall the passage verbatim"

A collaborative poem, playing with structure and sentiment. It tells a story of how the legacy of truth is constantly evolving. Words forever changing, living on longer than us. Poetry is spoken word, yet we have chosen to write our truths down with the knowledge that they will surpass us. We wanted this poem to be clever, forgive our lack of modesty here, but the poem repeats itself, the same sentiment but not the same words. It is not verbatim but then eventually, nothing ever is.

SUBVERSIVE MEDIA
PUBLICATIONS

www.ingramcontent.com/pod-product-compliance
Lightning Source LLC
Chambersburg PA
CBHW041306110526
44590CB00028B/4265